Amongst the Chaos

by

Gerard Gleeson

FOREWORD

As a resident of London, I have grown accustomed to the fast-paced way of city life. The daily routine of travelling across the city for client meetings. Business breakfasts followed by business lunches and drinks. The endless emails, the phone calls and meetings that carry on throughout the day and into the later hours. And in the late evenings, I would meet with friends or go on exciting dates with new girls all the time. Week after week, I would meet lots of new people from all around the world. This became part of my regular life and I loved it.

In the midst of this seemingly endless supply of novelty, distractions and dates, there was a sense of urgency — an urgency to keep pushing my work life and my social life to the next level. Always wanting more and to excel in life. It was addictive. Then, everything changed.

I hated the lockdown at first, the overwhelming feeling of claustrophobia set in. And this trapped feeling was intensified by the swarm of negativity, sensationalism and overall doom and gloom of the daily news. We were living in some kind of nightmare — in some dystopian future where human contact was reduced to WhatsApp, phone calls and video chats, leaving the safety of our homes only for supplies and quickly scampering back.

It was during one of the most devastating pandemics of modern times and craziest times of my life that I reignited my passion for writing. As the habits and daily routines of not only Londoners, but people around the world came to a dead stop, it also signalled a time to take a step back and reflect on the last few years of this fast-paced city living.

I am truly appreciative and grateful for the life I have built since I moved to London over seven years ago. However, life moves pretty fast. Not many of us hit pause long enough to reflect on where we are and where we are going in life. As for myself, I had been entangled in this modern-day predicament of constantly looking forwards. I was guilty as charged. I hadn't taking any time to reflect on the chaos of my life and how I was living day to day.

After the first couple of weeks of lockdown, I made peace with the situation. I realised it was completely out of my control and that I had to make the best of it. I knew this would be a true test of will and character for myself and the people around me. I saw one massive upside. What's the one thing that we never have enough of in life? Time. Now, there was no daily commute, no travel, no bars, no restaurants and no socialising. But suddenly, there were many more hours in the day.

You could fill your time with jigsaw puzzles and quizzes. You could binge-watch a series or, you could make the most of it. Your daily thoughts and actions can either bring you closer to a better version of yourself or they could leave you stagnant, stale and just going through the motions. These daily habits will either bring you closer to your goal or push it further away. It's as simple as that. You can live your life in fear and negativity. You can fill your head with a constant supply of what the mainstream media and press has to offer, or you could look inwards and focus on laying the brickwork to build up the house of your own mind. After a few more weeks in lockdown, I settled into a positive schedule. I thoroughly enjoyed my daily workouts. I went for long walks in nature that gave me plenty of time to reflect, tap into my creativity and to observe and learn new things. I also started reminiscing, too. I started missing my family and friends and, as these feelings grew stronger, I spent time looking through old notes on my phone.

For years, I have kept notes on various apps detailing my to-do lists, goals, notable quotes, song lyrics and various snippets on topics that I wanted to learn more about. Amongst the endless notes, I started finding poems that I had written on the go a few years ago — lots of poems.

I noticed though that I had not written anything in over two years. In looking back through these poems, I noticed that some were laughable and simplistic, some were just okay but some — some of these poems were very inspirational. When I read them a flood of memories came back.

It seemed not long ago that I would get a burst of inspiration and whip out my phone and jot the idea down quickly. I had forgotten this practice and left it aside.

Ideas and inspiration can be fleeting and if you don't get them down hastily, they often disappear forever. Poetry felt natural to me and the ideas flowed thick and fast. I have lived a full and colourful life so far, and this has provided me with quite a lavish banquet of ideas and experiences to draw from.

With this surge of inspiration, I began writing every day, noting every idea and bit of inspiration as soon as it came to mind. After a few weeks, it became an obsession. I was consumed with writing daily.

It tapped into a part of me that I hadn't known before. I was overwhelmed by how a few words on a page started to bring forth such strong emotions and memories. More so, it pushed me to work harder toward my aspirations. Before I knew it, I had written over fifty poems. Then the idea of possibly making a book didn't seem so far off — or out of reach. Then suddenly, I had some crazy days and nights when I got into a full flow state. For me, this was a state that can only be likened to a hypnotic trance. Many nights, I shrugged off sleep, possessed by a lyrical frenzy that kept me up past two or three o'clock in the morning. One day into a long night, I wrote a personal record-setting eleven poems. The intensity of emotion and adrenaline that filled this explosion of creativity is unforgettable.

In school or during formal educational, the idea of writing a book seemed foreign. I didn't necessarily excel at school and the concept seemed so far out of reach. The experience of writing this book has truly been an amazing journey. When you forget to eat. When the tea goes cold on the counter. When you stay up late into the early hours of the morning, completely engrossed in an almost magical outpouring of your own mind, your time in life takes on new meaning.

This kept me going throughout the pandemic and it brought me great happiness each day while the world around me was torn apart by fear and burdened by negativity.

Words are extremely powerful. They can evoke the strongest of memories. They can provoke even stronger emotions in people. We all hold stories and lessons inside of us that we should share with one another. Life is a full spectrum of emotions that we experience together and here, I hope you will enjoy the poems, life lessons and stories in this book.

TABLE OF CONTENTS

Amongst The Chaos

Lost in thought,
The depths of my mind.
All day I walk these corridors,
Leaving ideas behind.

Chaos

Amongst the chaos
I find my peace
Over the valleys
Through the trees

Shoulders back
Eyes a gaze
Leave the world
On its knees

Control the direction
Of what will be
Amongst the chaos
I find my peace

Through my dreams
Piece by piece
I will imagine
Then I will truly see

For what I see in the distant haze
Will soon be reality
Amongst the chaos
I find my peace

Don't forget
Who you were, and what will be
There's no-one else
Who see's things the way you see?

And if it becomes
Too much for me
I will remember,
This was always meant to be

My mantra on this journey,
Freeing me from the deep
Amongst the chaos
I find my peace

Empty Streets

Clear mind
Time to focus
Time to grind
Work harder
Leave them behind
Nowhere to be
But a fast stride
Empty streets
Clear mind

Dress your best
Even if nobody sees
Clean house
Purer mind
Good strut
Self-pride

Laser eyes
Stare them down
But be kind
Be assertive
Don't remind
Healthy hair
Sharp mind

Have passion
But don't rely
Work smarter
Don't be sly

Full life
Full mind
Empty heart
Left behind

Small win
Energised
Real smile
Solid vibe
Live it large
Don't deny

Don't be late
Never too early
Be just on time
Empty Streets
Clear mind

Beneath a Steel Sky

Beneath a steel sky
Our world has changed forever now
I am at peace regardless
I hope you are too.

Are we now as predictable
As all these machines?
Some of us having less soul than them
The false gold still keeping us keen.

I appreciate a cloud now
A blade of grass in my hands
The complicated man, moved back to a simpler time.

Life has fewer demands
Now a day is a week
And weekends are just the same
Time draws longer now, but I am never bored.

I hope you don't believe it all
I hope you found a real side
Most are trapped now, but
Not all of us, in mind.

Smile for the camera
Your dear Queen's CCTV
We're freer than them, overseas
We still have humour and free speech.

Beneath a steel sky
Propelled in a metal tube
I'll walk my own pace, take my own path
Which one will you choose?

PARK LIFE

You took me on an adventure
They say third times a charm
We walked so many thousand steps
The glare of the sun to disarm

Breaking rules on lockdown
Not a care in the world
I forgot all about this crisis
The daily stories that were told

A million perspectives
As far as the eye can see
10 million colours
Of just a leaf on a tree

A million viewpoints
Of a few branches on a tree
As pure as crystal
Patterns never before seen

Perfectly imperfect
The way it's meant to be
All the colours of nature
A personal palette just for me

A thousand tones of the sun
Smiling back at my soul
Important but insignificant
Taking me out of this claustrophobic hole

A headstand in the park
A dog smiling back at me
Everything will be fine
They are trapped, I am living free

In the Park

I'll meet you in the park now
Over the fields
Beneath the comfort of the imposing parental tree

I'll meet you in the park now
You will be safer outside
No confinements here

I'll meet you in the park now
Drop the red pin
And I'll be late but I'll be there

I'll meet you in the park now
It's a place of joyful possibility
The new place to be

I'll meet you in the park now
Finally, its fully appreciated for its worth
A sidecar of the past

I'll meet you in the park now
So many to discover
They were there all along, but you didn't bother

I'll meet you in the park now
Share a story, share a beer
A circle of characters, weekend updates to hear

I'll meet you in the park now
Share an idea, share a dream
Have another beer, together we watch the sun gleam

I'll meet you in the park now
Clearer mind, cleaner air
I don't miss the old. I'd rather be here than there.

I miss my family, I miss the air, I miss my home.
I miss my people who long to roam.
You're always with me, everywhere I go.
An Irishman is never alone.

EIRE

I miss the pure cold air, inhaling deeply as I descend Ryan's
Flimsy narrow ladder.
The smell of silage, the cows all cheering my name.
The most authentic people you'll ever meet.
A different accent around every corner, yet Irish all the same.

The familiar voice, smile and wink at passport control.
Slang words you'll never find in any dictionary.
Slagging battles with the lads, who will get the victory?
GAA, rugby and cold creamy pints.
House parties and morning sessions, days into nights.

The big fry up with pudding, two white and two black.
The streets so quiet, a welcome break from the chaos.
The forgotten name you haven't seen in years.
Welcome home, great to see you kid, when you going back?

The next generation on their big night out.
Making you feel older, yet youthful again.
The memories of each shop, each street with dual names.
The school full of old stories, you used to partake in.

I miss my family. I miss my home.
No matter where in the world, I'll find my own.
You're all my friends, with a welcoming smile.
That part of me is always here.
An Irishman is never alone.

Cliffs of Dunlicky

Standing on the jagged rock, 45 degrees.
It's all in the hips, but my god it will test your knees.

The vicious sea breeze can be deafening.
Below the imposing seals are waiting,
Black cartoon eyes looking up.
Full of bristled whiskers, both smiling and heckling.

The cliffs of Dunlicky,
The height of madness.
The day we filled bin bags and huge buckets.
Over 150 between the four of us.
The seals chasing the mackerel.
And our shiny, feathered mini harpoons chasing them.
A new meaning to cat and mouse.

And us to each other,
"How many can you lift?"
My forearm straining under the might of heavy hooks.
6 dancing fish and a forearm like Popeye's.

The howling wind could cut you in two.
Mesmerised by the piercing sun, daydreaming.
The perfectly straight endless line of the horizon.
Hips ripped sideways by the catch, snapped back to reality.

Washing the plunder of the day towards the mainland,
In a shallow dark pool of tiny marine life.
The opportunistic seagulls gathering a crowd,
Waiting for their cut of the loot.
Holographic scales shining and calloused hands
Covered in blood and guts.

The old run-down chipper on the way home,
A nod to the past.
A hard day's graft, well earned.
A filthy, greasy, battered sausage and chips.
A salty feast for salty dogs,
A feast for salty lips.

Cigarettes and Poker Chips

Cigarettes and poker chips
My father celebrating loudly across the room
Embroiled in separate circular wars on the felt
Banned from an all-family table
Nodding to each other, see you in the final one soon.

The quaint old fireside lights up the cottage pub
Limestone blocks of pure Irish charm
The old man in a dusty cap clutching his black medicine
Alone in solace, deep in thought at the bar
Cigarettes and poker chips engulf the room.

I'm 24 now
But I feel like a boy amongst men
Take shit from nobody
A fearless naivety that wears thin
I'll bully them all if they come after me.
Don't show any weakness. I'm all in.

I am hard to read
In and out of the game
But who's fooling who?
I hit a lucky flop, conquering my opponent
The table gets slammed in vain.

Cigarettes and poker chips
My father four seats from me
We're not here for the money
We want your head too
It's a sickening game of no mercy.

Play the player not the cards
Risk it all for glory of the felt
Take no prisoners in this game
Not even those closest to you.

NYC

An Irish man's debut in NYC
A fiery, bearded McGregor wannabe
The year was 2016
And a fine Summer it was to be.

The streets so wide, more chill than London
Taxis dirty, not so yellow
Steam rises from the rock
The constant noise of traffic.
Nothing here seems mellow

"Free fireballs" said, my new friend to me!
The only real Irish in this dive of a place.
Sold to the highest bidder, and
They too, by the glass, selling my identity.

Nothing is real, in this metroplex pharmacy
An episode of this fictitious soap is an hour, a day?
They all claim heritage when they hear me talking
But it's all a ruse, don't you see?

I'm the man today, but a company one
First taste of the high life, all expensed
An Irish rogue's adventure
This lads first time in NYC.

I walk towards the sun,
To keep myself blind.
I avoid the shade now,
The shadows of my mind.

WITHIN

I'll level any woman, any man.
Test you every day.
All you've got to do,
Start the first strained rhythm.
The toll bridge of the body,
Make your bones pay.

Grip like the claw of an eagle,
Expel your demons of negativity.
Win the war of hesitation, the excuses,
The battle within.

Just pick it up and swing. Your power, your might.
Fight for your future self,
Ignore the false mind.
Trigger your hunter, your fight or flight.

The war begins in your inner world.
There's noise around, the clangs the grunts, the roars.
All around you internal battles unfold.
Sweat drips into your eyes, but some have given in.
Some still wanting more.

Win the war in here, outside will always seem tame.
Master your body or the mind will master you.
Surprise yourself, your untapped capability.
Always dwelling inside.
Unleash the inner turmoil, no excuses.

Let the body lead the mind.
Power on through.
Always doing what you think you can never do.

Bad Morning

On another planet
The wrong side of the bed
Dizzy and confused, off balance
Throat laced with dry lead

Shuffle to the toilet out of sync
Can't even find the light
Stand up and balance
Let the magic take flight

Pour the black potion
Forget the white twice, so perplexed?
Look at the fridge in a daze
This wasn't the start you would expect

There's something you forgot
But you've forgotten that too
You're missing a sock
And can't find a shoe

At an ungodly hour
You fell into bed
No time for breakfast
The scramble's in your head

A write-off morning, that will tease you more
It will swing at you with hooks and test your grit
Don't take it personally
It's just the way of the universe, doing its bit

BIRDS

Like an eagle
I swoop
I sweep away your dreams.

Like a falcon
I claw
I tear at your emotional seams.

Like a hawk
I descend
I take away what you need.

Like a crow
I will stare
Deep at your insecurity.

But you'll never win
I was born without sin
A lion and a lioness
My roar is deafening.

So, what now
Is that all you got?
I'll lick my wounds
I'll plot my next hunt
This jungle is my plot.

If you are breathing
You are winning

Still in the race
Never give up
Yours truly
Just a person talking,
To a mirror
A crazy determined face.

Two Sides

Introvert or Extrovert?
EN or INTP?
A walk in an empty park
A silent cup of tea?
Staring into space
Please don't talk to me

A walk on stage
An emulation of someone else
A forced smile and speech for praise
A handshake and pat on the back
Thoughts finally let out of their cage

A clang, a bang a solid melody
Another late night spent inside an unwritten symphony
A door locked, a legacy to create
Eyes a million miles away, no love but no hate

A circle of laughter
Improvised and acted out with my hands
They love this authenticity
It's getting late, are there any more cans?

A long walk to nowhere
Entertainment of the mind
I am poor, but truly rich
All at the same time

Handshakes around the room
Clinking of the glass
The chameleon has come out again
How long will he last?

Chair rolled back and stood up proud
Art bouncing around the room
Smiling ear to ear, a good feeling inside

This month's masterpiece
Your thoughts through a speaker
The inside unveiled soon to the public
Nothing left to hide

No Doubt

I'll write about how I write
While I'm writing
And thinking

I'll see what you think
What you've thought
Before you start blinking

I'll puzzle you now
Before you've even questioned
Or thoughts start linking

I'll put rips in your sail
I'll put holes in your bow
When it was never sinking

I'm unwritten
I'm unspoken
Negativity always slinging

I'll punch
Before a fight was provoked
I'll leave you breathless and swinging

I'll cripple you
The strongest of runners
Before you even know you're limping

I'll silence all words
Before they have formed
Or have sunk in

For those that ignore
I'll never leave you
Forever I'll be bringing

I cannot be beaten
But just remember

Always, at all times
One of us is winning

The Narrative

Don't let the liars and thieves fool you.
If you are blind, they will rule you.
Be a prisoner set free, in body
And the fortress of your mind.

Don't blindly repost to get off the hook.
Don't just parrot what was said.
There's multiple sides and opinions.
Don't be a beacon of today's fake news,
Echoing the trash you have read.

The hobbyist conspiracy theorists.
The wannabe statisticians.
The street-smart realists,
More revenue for them though.
Clicks are today's currency,
A scandal that's worth millions.

Systematic or emblematic?
Opinions spreading like a wildfire.
Based on no research, completely erratic.

You don't have to be a pastor,
For the ministry of truth.
Open your mind and search, look closer.
Find the real meaning, be Illmatic.
Find the truth in you.

Love the work, love it's worth.
Distractions everywhere, interfering.
Slowing down the train.
Learn to love it daily, the rest leads to pain.

THE WORK

The work comes first, always.
Remember this — the work must come first.

A shovel. A fist. A pen.
Do it your way, from the start.
Do it with effort, from the heart.
Do what excites you
And never force through a day.
Watch the fragments of time,
Hastily melt away.

The work comes first, always.
Remember this — the work comes first.

Passion is for romance.
Obsession is key.
Sleep is overrated, and I've no time
To read what your messages said.
I'm busy as always,
Relentless. Rest when you're dead.

The work comes first, always.
Remember this - the work must come first.

No time for nonsense
Or vague chit chat.
I'm stirring an alphabet potion

In this bubbling vat.
Bit of me, bit of them, bit of this, bit of that.

The work comes first, always.
Remember this – the work comes first.

The Mantra

Work smart, play hard,
Take on the world

Read books
Create looks
Put your intentions out there.
Watch it all unfold

Fake it
Make it
Be relentless
Be bold

The chaos and the order
Take on what each day brings
Don't ask for permission with ideas
Don't do what you're told.

If you follow, you'll always be led
Happiness isn't out there
It's all in your head.

Go forth and prosper
Like we are all born to do.
Conquer yourself, know what's true.
If you're not where you want to be
More work needs to be done.

It never ends.
There's always the next battle.
It's yours to be won.

5AM

The cool silence of morning.
The calendar of confusion.
A rhapsody of birds, loud and in sync.
The crow stands alone and proud,
Does he know what day it is?

The forced enthusiasm of an early head start.
The only one in the world awake.
Frowning at the white sun like a doctor's penlight.
London's morning call.
The mouthy Jack Russell is disturbed.

Silence replenishing the mind,
A break from the chaos.
Morning sounds begin to emerge from their slumber.
Helicopter circling, but for what purpose?
A child roars outside with enthusiasm.

The birds repeat their anthems louder.
The scaffolding clunks in the distance.
It's 8AM now, over the opaque blue sky.
My solo heartfelt work is done.
Before this crazy city has begun.

Dear Trees

A genius for two minutes.
But that's all I need.
Tapping the phone and typing frantically.
Possessed, ideas to seed.

It consumes me.
It fuels me.
So erratic. Hidden from the world now.
Nobody's allowed to see.

Mental chaos in solitude.
An introverted extrovert.

A whispered Irish accent.
A hushed soliloquy.

I already have too many passions
But this was unexpected for me.

I don't feel like a fraud.
It's a form of therapy, a self-enquiry.

A seed from yesterdays bucket.
Planted now forever.

One day I'll hold them all dear.
Branches of a thin white tree

I do not fear death.
But I do, a deathbed regret.
Life is a blink of an eye.
One day forever closed, lest you forget.

Concept

5 years old you left me,
I didn't understand.
I was just excited to be off school.
I didn't know where you went.
I couldn't hold your hand.

Everyone's so sad.
But still a beaming smile for me.
A young boy happily oblivious.
Around him misery.

Someone has left this world
And onto the next.
I didn't understand it then.
Where did he vanish to?
It still leaves me perplexed.

The room's so dark and silent
Standing to the side like divine statues,
Hands clasped and heads bowed.
Outside sunny and vibrant.
The birds all singing proud to me.

Running and laughing with unknown kids outside,
In the soaring summer sun.
That day I learned about life's contrast.
Death, I still haven't begun.

The Path

You were here
Now you're gone.
We were carefree children.
The four of us, best friends, same road.
Since we were all 7 years old.
Playing army in the woods until dark.
Summer's playing football in the sun.

It had been so many years
Since you moved away.
Still talk about those times with the last remaining one.
He's finally left the road too now.
And I'll never forget that day.

A river or a noose,
This was your path to choose.
I don't know where you are now
But I was as lost as you.
And I'll always wonder, what was loose.

But I know you're not in pain,
Wherever you may be.
I hope the food is great there.
And until we meet again
That's good enough for me.

The pleasure was all mine.
See you in the next one.

And I'll always remember
No pain, just a cheeky smile.
You shined brighter than the sun.

SCATTERED

Throw me to the sea,
Remember the hair at its best.
I'll be late anyway,
Never still.
The wild ocean never rests.

Throw me to the sea.
Wood never lasts.
I don't need a priest on call.
An awkward whisper,
In darkened, dreary rooms full of shaken hands.

Feed me to the salty deep
I'll surf my way home.
Have a pint or 10, in my honour.
God knows, in my life the bottle I have known.

"I'll sleep with the fishes "
Under an Irish reef.
But just like Sebastian
I'll have a party under the sea.

Throw me like a frisbee, smile.
Let me feel the breeze.
I'll fly to the sun,
I'll do as I please.

Throw me to the sea.
I have everything I need.

No need for doom and gloom.
Love always, it's been a blast.
I'll see you all very soon.

V.W.

You showed me art, creativity
An older perspective
An electronic, musical brilliancy

We were kings at 10
Producing dance anthems for free
Firestarter's, pellet guns and climbing trees

Then a misunderstood misdemeanour
A hard past that was unseen
Always a smirk
A smart answer for everything

You taught me a lot
Sparked a thousand ideas
That you'll never get to see

I carry your memory
Always-high tempo
I'll forever keep that rebellious energy

We went our separate ways
Life does that, now I foresee
I'll cherish those days, creating magic on the PC

I thought you were well
You always tried to hide it
We almost found the secret, to Monkey Island.

The fights we started
We were the best rival gang
The Irish version of Stand by Me

Now I'm in the film's ending
Looking up, reminiscing and typing
Staring at words on a screen

I'll never forget, the day they told me
Been far too many years my friend,
Another soul taken by the sea

Requiescat

To all those that have passed
Long may their fond memories last
Great impact they did have
Requiescat to you
Let's all raise a glass and salute.

You meant everything to us.

Your best smile, that favourite decade.
Thriving and in your prime
Many great stories, a legacy that lives on
A beautiful reverie.
The birds still sing around you
Lessons passed on; souls grown
A carving on a rock
Can't tell your true story.

Gone but not forgotten
A tattoo on our mind
Imprints left behind
The influence is clear.

Never forget
With every breath
Memories held dear.

Always here
A wave, a memento
A passing reminder of a moment in time.

Always and forever
I hold you close
Never forgotten
You were the best, may you rest
Requiescat.

Only those that improve you.
That fuel you and move you.
Together rising up, only seeing the real deal.
In tandem, dreams you will pursue.

BFF

Best friends forever,
A hidden language.
In-jokes and funny glances, only we can understand.
Stories going back years, they know it all.
There's comfort in that, the honest vulnerability.
All of your insecurities, your secrets, your fears.
The fun the laughter, the hugs and many tears.

Love them for who they are.
And what they soon will be.
Quirks and flaws are like bingo balls.
What number will you both draw today?

A familiar face, no matter where you are in the world.
Always there to guide you, to bring you back to reality.
Nobody knows you better, remember that.
Coming up together, the highs and the lows.
They've seen your flashes of glory,
They've seen you take life's harsh blows.

We've smiled until our face's went numb.
Together we've plotted, planned and tried.
Laughed so hard together we cried.
Birthdays, weddings, small wins and all the rest.
Many more years to come,
You my friend are the best.

THE GANG

The gang. The crew.
We have travelled so very far.
A multicultural pick and mix.
The A-team.
The light to my obnoxious cigar.

My biggest supporters
And I'm always there for you.
The good and the bad.
Always so much laughter
Always a new view.

We've seen the sun go down in Serbia.
Driven boats off the coast of Italy.
The beauty of Croatia on a mountain drive.
Easier to meet abroad these days, all scattered.
Too caught up with the busy London life.

From the New Year's snow in Berlin.
To strobe lit nights in the heart of Ukraine.
We share our joy, our energy.
We help each other's pain.
We disagree on music,
We wind each other up.
Each other's harshest critic.
The whiskey pregame drinking, in a McDonald's cup.

Always up for adventure.
I'll say yes to every trip.

Too many countries to count.
Our bond will never slip.

We will grow older, maybe wiser?
Already all a great success, no regret.
One day I'll race you in my Zimmer frame.
Who will take my next bet?

Unique

They love you for the little things,
Uniqueness is a virtue.
Quirkiness is actually endearing.
Remember the self is always coming through.
It should never have a curfew.

Authenticity is key.
Don't hide behind the miniature glass screen.
The world is full of actors, be counted for the real you.
Don't be a forgettable absentee.

Any fool can detect a lie.
They love you for what's really true.
Never forget my friend, you can hide in the shadows.
But the light is always shining through.

Nobody can love a fake ego,
Only authenticity.
Be your best, tell them all your worst.
Throw it all out there like free money.
Be not what they want,
Be what sets you free.

Militia

My thoughts in isolation
But my army's all intact
Some soldiers, some mercenaries
All bonded by a pact

Some medics, some lieutenants
The enemy has been tracked
There's strength in our numbers
Not fiction, just a fact

I'll check in with my troops
See what work there's left to do
I'll refine your battle plan if you need help
I'll demonstrate what's true

Some snipers, some specialists
My personal platoon
Putting in the work we all are
Our next mission will come soon

Always ready and supporting
Strong opinions to bear
A scaffolding of opinions
The only ones that truly care

A wave is never smooth
But I will always find the shore
My armada is behind me
That's all I need and more

Peace

My friend Lily
Darkest and deepest green
Leaves like waves of nature's silk
Overreaching for the speck of light
Roots like an endless octopus
An army of white, soil speckled limbs
Arms up in celebration

Too shiny to be real
The tallest purest white flower
Like an angel on a Christmas tree
Delicate pale sail, green veins
Glowing in the sunlight
Overflowing like a Basset Hounds ear

Flower like a paper arrowhead
Guarding the jagged yellow mine
Seed in all its bright glory
Protected by your sail
Revealed in its own time

So temperamental
Rising and falling over time
Waving your silk white flag
Natures truce of peace

The most flamboyant of my children
My friend Lily
Needy for attention

You stand out, loud and proud
Proudly above the rest

What's a girl to do?

Prayer

I said a prayer for you
That to yourself, you will be true
That your light will shine
Be more than, just a hue

I said a prayer for you '
That things will change
For the better, I promise
More than just a few

I said a prayer for you
That times will change
Soon luck will come,
Your deserved breakthrough

I said a prayer for you
That you will be enlightened
And that all your pending dreams
Will soon come true

I said a prayer for you
That you will be surrounded
By love and support, always
To guide you through

I said a prayer for you
Something greater
Something higher
To reach and pursue

I said a prayer for you
Know that I'm there for you
Be happy, be safe and remember
To yourself always be true

Family is everything,
Great comfort and love it brings.
Our own nest we all long to build,
In it the birds always sing.

Super S

I followed you to London
Flattery at its finest
A borrowed rave cassette tape
But that album in 97′ defined it

Staring at the skyline of offices
From Victoria's dome
This is what you pictured long before you left
Now staring out from within, a long way from home

I try to find the balance
But the best balancer is you
Thank god I'm younger
Time to catch up, a new lavish London life to pursue

You had an arrival
The most beautiful of girls
Then along came her sister
A house full of gymnast's poses and twirls

Career and family life
The standard was set
The juggle of London life
Mixed with a countryside sunset

I have a few years
To emulate and spin
Within a family of determination and success
You're the first to win

G.G.

My father
The Limerick man
Older now, I truly realise
You are a piece of me.

The gambler, the gardener
The rule breaker
Down a ladder, up a roof
Unbreakable is he.

Psychology master
An eloquent artist
A true extrovert, but always caring
Now I'm on the same path too.

Same name, different way
Once rivals
We are both free creative thinkers
Authentic and true.

Every day I'm passing on your lessons
Remembering what you've said
We'll have a pint and a gamble
Share todays tips that you've marked and read

A fine poker player and sportsman
On the field and off
Always the best humour
Cracking jokes off the cuff.

One day I'll pass on the lessons
That your father passed on to you
A wise man creates a wiser child
A piece of me, a piece of you.

LEOPARD

My mother leopard
Prints adorn her palace
Always deep in thought, hard at work
Darkest tea in your animal printed china cup

The rhythm of the needle
Effortless and rhythmical skill
There's mystery in that mind
That unmatched work ethic, that powerful will

Stylish and elegant
Not a rose without thorns
Graceful in your composure
But don't cross her or she'll roar

A tasteful home
The carefully mismatched kitchenware
Skillfully selected fabrics
An ongoing design love affair

Thoughts always forming
Soon to be resolved
A puzzle and a mystery
Hard to figure out

Growing young gracefully
Always unapologetically you, saying what you see
Always meaning and care in everything you do
To everyone you meet, the family and me

And as the years go on
In myself, some of these traits I see
A deep thinker with the sharpest tongue
Always thinking of everyone.
Selfless, determined as can be.

JO

The middle child, the creative one
You used to push me
Down the stairs

Luckily, I had a safety net
Cocooned in a pillow and its case
It was fun for a dare

You used to push me,
Around in my blue plastic car
Pick me up when I fall

Now you're pushing them
The blondest of boys
The proudest mother of them all

Best of friends they'll always be
Girls wreck your head
But it's houses for the boys

The troublesome twosome
My little buddies
I'll supply the Uncle energy and toys

You have a proud father
But also include me
Your little brother, now a man
I'll push you if you need

Bernard

Arnie in a movie
Terminator, sometimes on two wheels
But you are what's real
A man made out rods of steel

More surgeries and setbacks
Never a bad word to say
How can anyone complain
If they lived an hour of your day

The most hardworking couple
Positive as can be
My childhood in the sewing room
You both smiling and carefree

You can't see as well now
But I know you are as lucky as can be

My auntie, your daily sidekick
A heart of gold you can easily see

I look up to my father
And he speaks so highly of you

As tough as tough can be

To you from us both
You're the definition of resilience
A true hero, cruising out at sea

YEARS

My inspiration

46 years married
The rarest of unions
Opposites really do attract
The most inspiring thing I've seen

A shaky WhatsApp video call
Both interrupting each other, happy as can be
Finishing each other's sentences
Both thick as thieves

So masculine and so feminine
The best friends that will ever be
Looking after each other with balance
Always staying positive, young and carefree

You raised us so well
Over the years always re-inventing, working so very hard
A big gang of boisterous grandkids
A fantastic legacy to pass on, to nurture and to guard

Always in my thoughts
Filtering the lenses through which I see
From your only son
I'm as proud as can be

Long may it continue
The rarest of truths
46 years married, I still can't believe it
Two doves in cahoots

The wolf with no pack surrounding.
Wild dogs never enough, they can't compare.
Out on your own in the bitter snowy forest.
Howling louder than ever before.

LOST

The hunchback on the tube seat.
The disposable coffee cup.
The pizza box tumbling in the wind.
How badly have we fucked this up?

The child on the airplane
Clutching tightly at the iPad screen.
The person sleeping in the damp
Corner, ignored for eternity.

The large family at the restaurant
Who can't hold each other's gaze.
The one-click online order
A supposedly new phase.

The most beautiful scenery
A sunset so vivid and serene.
A moment of a lifetime missed
For a tiny screen.

A plethora of melody,
A rhythm in time.
Nobody's really there in the moment
Distraction not sublime.

Another chapter goes by
Wasting moments, wasting time.
By hours, by days lived out.
Of a fake life online.

Wash it Away

Swat it away, the angry vicious wasp.
Your validation based on fraud
Trying so hard to prove yourself
To an unworthy world.

Brush it off your teeth
Scrub harder and harder
Spit it down the drain
A bloody and messy spiral
Death to your big ego
Wash it all away.

Melt it like butter
Watch it turn burnt liquid brown
Throw it down the sink
Watch it crackle and spit,
Watch it plummet, watch it drown.

Dissolve it in water
Let it fizz and bubble
Disintegrating from your life.

Stub it out and stamp on it
Kill the burning flame
Brush away the ashes
And wave away the disgusting smoke.

Death to the big egos
Let the world wake up
You are a nuisance to us
All you have caused is pain.

Fidget Spinner

The Fidget spinner
Keep it spinning
Fast as it will go
A merry-go-round of materialism
No depth here, just superficial don't you know?

It will hypnotise you from the start
Watch it sway and spin
The silver halo putting you in a trance
Like magpies dreaming of a perfect nest.

Faster and faster
Keep the energy high
Don't stop to breathe, to appreciate
Chase the swipes, double taps and the precious likes

Always another one
Always wanting more
A daily targeted consumer
An illusion in packaging, making you ignore.

Try to keep up with the latest
It's a losing game
It will spin faster and forever
Gold wasted, thrown away in vain.

Some people never realise
Some people just don't come off
Like a greedy pig
Gorging on food, slowly drowning in its trough.

MASCULINITY

The masculine and feminine,
Role reversal gone wrong.
The conqueror and the nurturer.
Both misunderstood, do we now really get along?

A quiet desperation.
Afraid to look weak, to speak out, to call.
Silence is man's downfall.
The greatest killer of them all.

The only thing toxic is the food you eat.
Navigate the rabbit hole of lazy journalism,
Understand how it really works.
Go to university, take a coloured pill
Or get thrown the book in court.
A mad world where comedians are
The only ones saying the truth.

Ask yourself, is the effort worth the reward?
Sanctity no longer a necessity.
Believe in the individual when tarring with your brush.
Who invented these machines that protect you?

It's masculinity in crisis.
The woke, the weak, the eunoia of the rare.
Will you take the coloured pill, be a rebel without applause?
There are no feminists on a sinking ship,
The individual is the cause.

Excess

This life of excess
The expensed bar tab of fine craft gins
The roulette wheel of lust at your fingertips
The marbled hotel reception,
The purple velvet armchair all plush
50 years of cinema at a button push

The cocktail with a quirky twist, that belongs in the Tate
The expansive house with more TVs than people
The perfect wardrobe, more outfits than days in the year

The proud bookshelf, you will get around to read
The latest gadget, that will make your life easier
You just have to have it; this new one you really need

Thousands of photos on your phone
Yet you haven't printed one
Videos of concerts you will never watch
Your phone primed with content, before it had begun

The cupboard full of supplements for peak health
20 tabs of research, the ultimate top 10 tips.
No intuition to guide you.
An app for everything, even for your mental wealth.
No mind of your own, a planted media voice.

Voluntary simplicity.
Take off the blinkers of excess

Create space to learn more about yourself
Build relationships, not your profile.
Sort out the inside first, fix your broken house.
Don't be another mess, in this modern life of excess.

Turn words and thoughts into finished works.
Chase greatness, not the temporary fix.
Believe in your glory, always.
Some days true greatness, some days amiss.

The Light

I write deep into the darkness
But all the light is in me

I'm actually excited for tomorrow
A new momentum has its place instilled
Long may it last
This I did not foresee.

Will I be enlightened
A fraction of a second more
Will I succumb to procrastination?
Scrolling through the scandals
A wasted tale of lore.

Find your inner fight
Build it from a simple chore
Wear multiple hats, try them and see
Find an obsession to live and die with
The light is within all of you and me

It will strike you unexpectedly
At the strangest of times.
And you won't ever be fully ready
But you will always manage just fine.

Don't be afraid to start, weave your own tapestry of happiness
So absorbed in your craft, not caring what they think.
The tea always goes cold, abandoned on the countertop.
You forget to eat; you just don't realise.
You forget the world; you forget to blink.

Flow

I'm not a creative
This wasn't planned you see
There's something I found one day
It just flows out of me.

I wish I could predict it, bottle it and sell
It would turn me from head to toe into gold
Then my soul down a well
If the truth be told.

It's greater than any drug
One day you might know these ways
It's better than an icy breeze
On the most sweltering of days.

It summons up within me
But it's as fleeting as rain, as rare as Irish snow
I wish I could control it
When will you return? I have many seeds to sow.

Channel it and save it
Come back another day and show
You might have some magic there
When will it arrive again though? Never will you know.

Forever chasing each other, like so
Forever perfecting and refining
Nothing beats the flow.

THE NIGHT

Beneath the vivid moonlight, under the green canopy.
I work alone and undisturbed.
Deprived of sleep and lifting open heavy eyes.
Ideas come fast and shine, illuminating the night.

The city colder now, but a calm unrest.
The roars of the night-time defectors,
Limping hastily under street lamps.
Police sirens echo faintly in the distance. Engines rev.
Torn between my reverie and exhaustion.
I purposely dance between two opposing states of mind.
A personal creative experiment.

The repose of the dim moons cast.
My 5am start in reverse.
I fall asleep but jolt awake again, this time more awake.
The weak drone of delivery mopeds returning home.
Struggling to gain momentum.

I am an owl on a tree squinting.
Watching over my city.
Yawning like a silent lions roar wakes me up again.
Stuck halfway between today and tomorrow.
Neither night nor morning.
Still and silent.
Midway world.

The ding of an empty can,
Being kicked angrily down the street.
The faint street lamp across the road,
Hovering over the local park.
Pipes being lit in the nightly ceremony.
A pen, a glass pipe.
A lighter, candlelight.
We are both restless and relentless,
Looking for our fix tonight.

LUCID

They told me to smile
Smile large and bright.
I had forgotten the basics
Wrapped up daily, distant and in future thought.

They told me about
The playful curious child.
I saw past him everyday
I left him behind.

They told me you have love trapped within you
Don't hold back any longer, let it out.
Let go of pointless fear and anger
Melt away all your doubt.

They guided me gently
Told me I'd always be safe.
Soon you will wake up
And be ready for what you need to face.

Your problems are not real
They are all in your head.
Live it up and breathe gratefully
For soon you will be dead.

Look into their eyes
And see what they see.
They are all your personal threads
Your soul, a multicoloured tapestry.

DIRECTORS

Writing is the greatest
Confront your greatest fear
I can make you think a thousand ways
I can make you uncontrollably shed a tear

I can bring up vivid images
Of a distant future and the past
Try it someday
Make those fainter memories last

The great stories of a life well lived
The blind haze of a past romance
Loved ones you have lost
Society's contrast, your final dance

For we are all directors
Of a thousand screenplays

Everyone has a story
Everyone has those memorable days

Just try it and you'll see
Your own scrawling mental symphony

Better than any modern media
Just write it down and walk away

Let it out and leave it be
Leave it for another day

It can make you greater
Make you want to guarantee

Just start tomorrow
And surprised you will be

Words on a page
A glimpse of your mind, we can all see

Face your fears.
Don't run away for years.
Do you want to hang with stray dogs?
Or wrestle with bears?

ANCHOR

The anchor
Solid
Heavy
It pins me to the surrounding sea

It's imposing, unshakeable
If you need me come calling
In my beautiful boat I shall be

It's choppy
It's treacherous
Will they show me?
Or on my own will I see?

It's very simple
My anchor
My family
My friends
Me

I don't need a compass
A lighthouse
A treasure map
For they are all here with me

On my finger
A tattoo to remind me
On the daily, I see

I'll cross any ocean
Any time
Any weather
Together we can both be

I don't need a lighthouse to guide me
For we are all on this voyage
Together, out at sea

NUMB

They say ego is the enemy
But so are you, to me
You destroy lives
You make people think they're free

Numbness in bottle
Suppression at its best
Just keep them coming
Forget about the rest

What you chase away is seeking you
When you numb this moment, tomorrow is still there
Tell yourself a lie today
But soon it's a real truth.

Face your demons
Don't put them in a glass
Stand up and be counted
The negativity can always pass

Use it as a tool
But don't underestimate the power
A day wasted; the mornings lost
A long reflective shower

Be careful of your mood
It's amplifying effects
A double-edged sword
Take care you won't be vexed

Lack of judgment
Decisions made in haste
The answers lay not in a bottle
Thoughts just laid to waste

I hope you'll be okay
And time to your body will be kind
But always remember my friend
The glass is left behind

DEATH BEFORE SURRENDER

Within us
It will fuel you
Dowse you
Consume you
Flames are at your fingertips

Powerful and sure
Removing all necessities
No sleep, no satiety
Let them have false hope
A passionless society

Momentum like a rocket
Focus of a sniper
Fists clenched, power stance
Tongue out like an aboriginal dance

As you burn in flames
Incoming like an asteroid
Destroyed bridges left behind

A mindset that reigns glorious
Unbreakable
Soon victorious
Death before surrender

Will you run towards her in the rain?
Will you renounce the dark days, of lost love?
Spin the wheel of uncertainty again.
Dry off in the blistering sun, forgo all pain.

Black Velvet

Curvaceous seductress,
Unmistakably salacious in your ways.
Velvety, dark, smooth beauty.

Curves to die for.
I crave your vitreous and
Smooth skin, vivacious grin.

Leave my lips wanting more.
Mysterious shadowed enchantress,
Undressing before my eyes.
Too soon and our flame diminished.

Men queue for a mere sight of your grace.
A global temptress, a phenomenon.
They dream night and day of your embrace.

Cold at first, then warm to the touch.
A thickness and a thinness.
An orchestra on the palette.
A concert of violinists.

Playing on your harp of love,
Swirling from a thin cloud above.
Better for you than spinach.
My goodness my Guinness.

Opposites Attract

Words on a page
Thoughts in my bulb
The darkness of the night
The silence of the room

Awake with no reason
Unhappy and despaired
Everything going for you
Yet you still don't care

I want to be at peace
And silence this light
And wake up restful and rise
For an active minds a blessing
And a curse in disguise

I lay awake and wonder
How it's all played out
I'm only human
And my body of work
Sometimes I doubt

But when I doubt the most
And all seems lost
A spark arises
And ideas are laid down
So frantically at all costs

I give myself a headache
And the greatest joy too
I can entertain in silence
And uncover new truths

An introverted extrovert
Or is the opposite true?
I wouldn't change it for the world
I'd never be like you

ACES

I had to forget my self
To really find you
I had to see the unknown
To know that it's true

I had to let go
Falling backwards, eyes closed
I really let go
Don't second-guess me, I know

I had to look inside
And open the box
I had to throw away the wrapping
And break the locks

I had to trust
That everything will go well
I had to reveal it all
And let father time tell

I had to be taught
Things I already knew were true
You showed me a new side
I showed one only for you

I had to be patient
Play my cards close
Tell only those
That I love the most

I had to analyse and look behind
To find comfort in my mind
For I don't need aces anymore
Now I've got one of a kind

Out to Sea

Unravel
Down the rabbit hole again
Unravel to travel
We go

Down down
Deeper down
Uncover the toxic
Like the melting of snow
Let it go

Uncover and recover
From the past
Open wounds to heal them
But don't expect to heal so fast

Use your anchor
Your haven
To relax and let free
From the surrounding ocean
The storms you can see

Come on board
And look out in the distance
The sun is shining, it's glistening
Across the vast opaque ocean
Sometimes smooth, sometimes rocky
A beautiful boat we shall be

MUSE

You look at me with wonder
What craziness lies inside?
I have a touch of madness
Step in for the ride

Hair is getting longer
So feminine and fair
A natural selection
More and more you care

I'll bring you on an adventure
Inside and out
The silence and the chaos
The funny laughing pout

I'll show you more
Of what lies inside
The child and the grown up
Which one will he hide?

I'll aim higher and higher
And keep my passion bright
I'll try to show the best of me
A whisper late at night

I'll save you if you shall befall
But mistakes on your own you have to make
I'll be around if you call
And show you what is real, what is fake

The balance of two sides
Too subtle to understand
Just be by my side
For life has its many demands

I'll bring out something deeper
A black hat and a dove
I'll hold you for this moment
A hand inside a glove

Spin

The ice queen
The village girl
Two sides denied

Maybe I am blind
Or I just see what no one sees

I analyse and study
But it's natural with you
Smaller angles revealed over time
Like a diamond of truth

The mundane becomes a game
I'm calm as can be
The sides are more balanced
It's plain as day to me

The jagged edges slowly smoothed
The cracks fading away
The water washes through
A cooling tidal wave

You haven't been affected
It's refreshing to see

I spun the wheel
I placed my bets
It's green as grass can be

I walked home in the heavy rain.
My face cold, heart in pain.
I ran towards you, trying be fixed.
But I've never stopped running away.

The Shoehorn of Despair

Childhood friends, my sidekicks of a forgotten era.
We were wild boys back then.
The sign to the entrance of our road read:

Beware of the children.
The good times, the simplest of times
But outgrown now for sure.

My longed new profession overseas
Pathways lined with liquid and solid gold
The polished brass and white marble reception.
Everything progressing, but now the novelty has worn.
I can feel the unbearable tightness.

My younger cherish , I do adore
Blind love that will never see
But now it's just not the same anymore.
Growing pains are hurtful
And I need to grow more.

Barefoot and stranded
Or struggling in vain
A stamped heel in frustration.
A mismatch in denial – the cracked old leather.
An obvious pain.

Yet you try and force it
It has to be comfortable enough,
To handle life's wear and tear.
Hopefully you won't need it again,
The shoehorn of despair.

Missing

When will I stop,
Stop missing you.
Memories haunt my thoughts.
I wonder do I still spook you too.

Unanswered questions, an uneasy state.
When will I stop,
Stop missing you.
Traversing the arctic blizzard, around in circles.
My lips gone cold, quivering and turning blue.

The largest sweeping valley,
A tsunami couldn't fill.
Memento flashes from the smallest things.
Replaying the ideal scenarios with a false lens.
The highlights, lowlights, the showreel.

Sometimes laying alert in wonder,
An addictive reminiscence of good moments.
A fantasy or reality, a hidden epidemic.
Sipping from the chalice of regret.

The burden and the blessing,
Of the constantly active mind.
But the soul must grow, memories foregone.
Evolve, an accumulation of spiritual wealth.
The sweet and the bitter.
Life goes on.

Rent

Holding back a tear
A rainy nightclub queue
It's just gone New Year's
The countless sparklers waved in the bar
A cheer, a fake woohoo!

Don't dwell, dig it up and think
Of what you could and couldn't do
Victories and casualties of the heart
A battle that was worth it
And these days there is very few.

For all we have are moments
So enjoy them while you can
A smile and a memory
Lessons learned in a symphony
But never going to plan.

And always remember
You won't have all the answers
Its what you both had to do
It wasn't your entire fault
This just wasn't meant for you.

There will be another sunset
You will always smile again
It was real not fiction
You went all in on this bet
Now a new page to begin.

The present will pass
It now feels like an emotional lent
But until the next time
Remember,
Your heart must pay the rent.

What's the Reason?

They come into your life
Not for nothing
Reasons are defined

Some come to teach
Some come to test
Some come to preach
Some are just declined

Will they inspire you to greatness?
Will they be forgotten quickly?
Or just be left behind?

These reasons are also yours
And sometimes yet to be defined

Don't let the past judge you now
Who knows what lies behind?

A reason to meet
To greet
Be authentic
Be kind
Be open

Don't deny it
Who knows?
A door unopened
Your heart, a key of the mind

The Snow

Through the fields of Pripyat
I met a lone wolf in the backdrop of a dense forest
Kindred spirits staring each other down in silence
Both searching a wasteland for answers
A snow-filled empty despair

The metal siren
Watching over her boroughs
The army truck in a hurry to nowhere
Like a budget made-for-TV war movie

I feel as fun as this rusted fairground
Motionless since 86′
A heavy eyelash full of snow wakes me
Through the foggy trees I see movement.

Przewalski's horses
Running powerfully, running free
Life goes on, disaster or not
I smile inside

On top of this apartment complex of past lives
A rooftop view of the vast dystopia
A wasteland, yet a jungle
Full of hidden wild and thriving life

Through the perfect white fields
Houses of memories and lives lost

The snow makes the mundane glisten in beauty
I appreciate my locale more now
This wolf will soon howl again

BRIDGES

Burn all the bridges
Of roads leading nowhere.
Flashes of light, days gone by.
The warmth of the burning flames across your face.

The boats shimmer behind you.
Reflections on the water, illuminate the path ahead.
A wavy luminescent arrow pointing north
The compass of your new future.

A clear ending is your resolve.
Through the smoky haze you seek clarity
Being liked is overrated, having vision is not.

Crossing the cold water, in your lone birch canoe.
The flames crackle and roar. But not as loud as your desire
For wanting more, pastures new.

Paddling ferociously, long into the depths of the night.
A small candle to a burning bridge
To the highest of mountains we go.
A hero's journey to rewrite.

How long said the tortoise?
Soon! said the hare.
'I'm in no rush'
Said the wise old bear.

Lessons

School taught me nothing.
Life did.
I still didn't learn all my times tables.
You can memorise knowledge, but life requires wisdom.
A sip of whiskey and I'll tell you a hundred fables.

Kids teaching children.
Outdated words on a page, manufactured obedience.
Educate yourself on what's truly vital.
Today's world of distraction, the so-called information age.

Never mistake knowledge for wisdom.
Knowledge can be your livelihood;
The latter leads to a full life.
The theorists. The intellectual fakers. The wannabe sage.
There's more to life, look around and really see.
The realists, the action takers.
More than just theory, words on a page.

A prince and a pauper,
Student loans and debt.
Knowledge outdated before you begin.
Play to your own drum, your own rhythm.

School, a distant memory, knowing yourself now a lot more.
For we are all teachers, realise it or not.
Relationships, finance, the art of persuasion.
Self-awareness, unfortunately some have forgot.

Older now, you can be what you truly seek.
Build a bridge of wisdom to the soul,
And allow others to pass through.
Every day is a new lesson, teaching us all what's really true.

TODAY/TOMORROW

Today's Pain
Tomorrow's story
Next month's lesson
Books don't have all the answers
But one sentence can fuel you for years

Today's joy
Tomorrows question
Next month's goal
We are reaching out for gurus
But they never have the real answer

Today's confusion
Tomorrows disillusion
Next month's setback
Things appear smaller in the distance
When you push onwards

Today's meaning
Tomorrow's revelation
Next month's progress
Even a stray dog
Can teach you a valuable life lesson

Today's grind
Tomorrow's momentum
Next month's habit
Your best current work
Will be average and insufficient in the future

Today's warm bubble
Tomorrows trouble, day of slack
Be careful of your words in haste
They can rarely be taken back

Reflection

A time for reflection
But you didn't have time to think
Another chapter finished
Don't miss it
Don't even blink

Was this even me?
How far this has come
You pushed the character too far
But by god was it fun

Locked in a box now
What you thought matters
Is no longer more
But life goes on

Take stock and relax
Take a breath
Don't dwell on it too long
Take on the lessons and reflect

Another time for reflection
But you actually had time to think
Another chapter finished
I have reflected, learned my lessons
This time, I think?

THE DOORWAY

The yellow imposing Victorian front door,
A vintage marker of a moment in time.
A beautiful narrow awning, neither hers nor mine.
Steep white narrow steps ascending to a welcome seat.
Beside me the blondest of hair, ivory snow-white smile.
A quick stop for shelter that warped time,
Pouring our hearts out like the blistering rain outside.
The warmth of the feminine divine,
The finest late-night express wine.

Heavy topics deliberated but feeling light inside.
No words needed now, I'm without words observing.
It just feels right.
Moving freely across topics, across each other's minds.
So much wiser now but feeling like a teenager again.
The antique brass, the lions head door knocker.
Watching over the road, guarding us both.
Passion putting my soul and eyes in a spin.

Steep white steps ascending to the narrowest of seats
But the widest expression.
All the jewellery in the world, the finest restaurants
You can just forget.
We just need a concrete step, a charming smile
And a slim menthol cigarette.

A piggyback up and down the street.
The pouring rain in each other's eyes.
One legged squats on my bruised ankle,
Showboating for kicks.

Feeling powerful and strong as can be.
Strangers walking by bemused in the late of the night.
They slink home alone in defeat,
I'm king of my high throne of romance,
King of our narrow concrete seat.

The yellow door, stairs ascending to a new chapter.
Doorstep of a kiss,
Rain is natures romance.
Sprinkling its magical mist.
I feel alive again.
My heart starts up its engine again.
Oh, how these moments I have missed.

The Number

This is it
A marker in your life
You never thought it would turn out this way
Surprises and the like

A mirror of your forgotten reflection
And remembering the past
Don't look back too long
You've come so very far, so fast

A big moment in time
Or perhaps just another year to reveal
Don't dwell or make a fuss
At your age nothing's a big deal

You can't predict the future
Or forget about the past
All you have is smiles and memories
And my friend, long may they last

You're proud of yourself
Like a father of his son
A private screening of your own blockbuster movie
Is this really what you have become?

Don't hesitate or doubt
No need to conform
Let the masses chase their tail
For this purpose, you were born

We are ready for tomorrow
A new set of memories, not just another day
Don't sweat the small stuff
Let the chips fall where they may

Age is just a number – well that's what people say

One Tonne

One hundred poems
A wannabe Seamus Heaney
Like Jordan in the MLB
I'll swing and swing.

My name in a library
Written beneath a steel sky
What's the next endeavour?
Words or a great melody, only I will decide.

My mind in a hundred pieces
Scattered across the world
Calmer now and wiser too
Still looking for life's truth, the perfect word.

One hundred stories
Finished in a fish tank
Onto the next one
Even though my mind demands a hundred more.

What's next you ask?
One hundred women
And a hundred grand
It may be enough for the simple man. Not me.

But maybe, just maybe
Maybe this was it and more.

The Legacy

When I cease to be, I want a legacy
A fine body of work
This art is my only child for now
And I have a village full

What will last at least 100 years?
After the cold descent, all the dried tears?

But this work can live on
I always think of the end
When I'm at the beginning

My thoughts
Always a million miles away
40 years ahead
Or 3 behind

Death is a reality
I'll see the daily sunshine
But I won't be blind

Simple or complex
That's up to you, not me
I care about you
But I must keep building

Distant and always busy
One day you will see
And I'll keep adding bricks to it.

My future legacy.

FINITUDE

The finitude of life
Hands moving, yet it's indistinguishable
You can't see it, touch it or grasp it
Yet you value fool's gold above it.
We all seem to forget.

If the end was revealed to you
How would you now go about your days?

The cascade into the river runs dry
Yet you were thinking of the tide.
How will you blend the present and the future?
The toughest balancing act of our lives.

Wisdom remains timeless.
Will you now be happy?
Or live for the future?

The finitude of life
Forever in motion, day to night
Counting down, forwards or backwards?

Live it up
Live it well
Live it right
The finitude of life

ACKNOWLEDGMENTS

First of all, I would like to thank my wonderful family for always being there for me, for inspiring me and for having a great positive attitude. To my parents for instilling in me a solid work ethic, inner drive and for always holding yourselves to a higher standard. Most importantly for your great love and support, fantastic humour and for not taking life too seriously.

To my sisters who I'm always looking up to and trying to catch up with. It has been amazing to watch you both excel in your lives and then go on to have wonderful families. To see you both balance successful careers with being amazing mother's has been very inspirational to witness.

Thank you to my friends from all over the world, clients, colleagues, good friends, ladies and brothers. Shout out to the London gang that I have travelled the world with. We have had many crazy adventures across multiple countries, cities and festivals. It's crazy how we are all so different yet, we get on so well and learn a lot from each other. To all the lads back in Ireland who always bring me back down to earth and remind me of who I am and where I come from. Thank you for always welcoming me back home and for keeping me grounded.

All of you who have contributed to this book in some way, shape or form, thank you for being part of my life and my story. This book should help reveal who I really am a lot more and hopefully shows some different sides that I don't normally show the world. I hope that this book will help us understand each other more and strengthen our relationships. Thank you all for inspiring me and helping me navigate through life. I hope you are all healthy, happy and fulfilled in your life wherever you are reading this from in the world. And I raise my glass to you for many more good times and stories to come.

Love always,
Gerard

Amongst The Chaos

For permission requests and press,
the author can be reached via social media or email:
gerardthepoet@gmail.com

ISBN: 9798785233782 (Paperback)
ISBN: 9798785141155 (Hardback)

Instagram: @gerardspoetry
www.gerardspoetry.com

Printed in France by Amazon
Brétigny-sur-Orge, FR